MW00941649

1893 Chicago's Columbian Exposition

Arts & Culture from the Doorstep of the 20th Century

Michael Finney

ISBN: 9781082413582

Also available from the Chicago 1893 Project

Documentary Film

Soundtrack

Merchandise

Facebook

Twitter

Instagram

To preserving history.

1893 Chicago's Columbian Exposition

TABLE OF CONTENTS

Introduction to the Fair

Chicago's Columbian Exposition World's Fair was staged more than 125 years ago. During the second half of 2018, I published a long-form Twitter thread based on photos from an antique book of official government photographs taken to document and promote the event. There were also additional posts of supplemental content that connect the events of 1893 with today's world.

Like the space race of the 1960s, the Columbian Exposition was a catalyzing event which aided to guide the American psyche regarding technological progress. It single-handedly focused many communities' efforts and attention on one goal, which was itself an opportunity to display how profoundly people can work together to translate a vision into a reality.

Historically, it is a coda to the era of classical aesthetics that dominated architecture for centuries. Contemporary Chicago architects had begun to unleash skyscraping buildings onto the streets of U.S. cities, a style that would define skylines of the 20th century.

An architectural event at its heart, Director of Works Daniel Burnham (who was handed the reins of command thanks to his reputation amongst his peers) produced a platform for America's elite architects to bring their grandest visions to life using the most fantastic ideas and materials available in those times.

The grandeur of the Columbian Exposition was intended to overshadow the World's Fair held in Paris four years prior, during which Eiffel's Tower served as the entrance. Its design was futuristic for the age and became iconic in minds around the world as an emblem for the "City of Light".

While many images show the incredible detail of the works on display, these aerial images truly do justice to the scope of the civil engineering and landscaping required.

The western entrance of the Midway Plaisance was about a mile west of Jackson Park. In this image you can see buildings that illustrate the structural aesthetics of Germany, Istanbul, and China.

The Grand Basin was a vast central water feature that measured 1300' long by 300' wide. Standing at the edge of the Basin allowed attendees to take in many of the prominent buildings of the Fair.

Daytime was for crowds while nighttime allowed facilities and faculty to rest, resetting for the following day. This engraving (as the era-bound book refers to the images) depicts the Grand Basin lit by electric light with a judicious helping of embellishment throughout from the publishers of the book.

What had been only a few years prior a boggy swamp on the south end of town was now a place of fantasy. The country had entered an economic panic in the early 1890s, a reprieve from the financial woes was a psychologically benefit. In fact, thanks to the construction demands in Jackson Park, the Chicago region's economy faired better than those of other cities.

In the moonlight, the Great Basin reflected enough light for an official Fair photographer to capture a small amount of detail in the silhouettes of the surrounding buildings. These photos were often the only views non-attendees would see, since there was a $2 fee to bring a camera inside. Rentals inside the park were an expensive option too.

This view of the Grand Plaza captures a number of wonderful feature elements such as the Electricity Building and the MacMonnies Fountain of Columbia.

The Columbian Fountain, which was sculpted by Frederick MacMonnies was the feature fountain of the 1893 World's Fair. While Columbia is seated atop the display, figures adorned the rest of her ship as well such as Time, Music, Industry, Science and Agriculture - to name a few.

The photographic anthology's creators took some artistic license with the images in it. Below is the basin around the MacMonnies fountain with the cascades "enhanced" via illustrative flourishes for visual effect. The Agricultural building is in the background.

The mechanical fountains put on grand displays both day and night thanks to electric light. Both of the circular pools shown over the previous pages are flanking the MacMonnies fountain which was crafted of plaster in Paris and then carefully transported to Chicago.

Electric fountains like this were new attractions in the Gilded Age. The mechanical components were delicate and required regular maintenance to keep running. When the fountain was playing it was capable of an amazing display of formations in a multitude of colored lights.

An aquatic theme prevailed throughout the Columbian Exposition, while artistic features adorned the buildings and waterways in every direction. In front of the Southern Portal was an obelisk flanked by lions similar to those modeled by Edward Kemeys, who is responsible for the pair in front of the Art Institute of Chicago which opened in 1893 as well but is not located in Jackson Park.

If you ever want to see one of the lions for yourself, you only need to head to Michigan Avenue and stop in front of the Art Institute. A pair was created just for the museum and guard the main entrance of the building to this day, though they are not the ones originally located in Jackson Park.

Chicago is home to many museums throughout the city. Three classics can trace their existence back to 1893. This first structure began its life as the World Congress Auxiliary of the World's Fair Columbian Exposition. Immediately after the close of the event on November 1st it was repurposed as the new home of the Art Institute of Chicago. For many years it was one of only a few permanent fixtures in Grant Park.

The collection that launched the Field Museum of Natural History in 1893 included many artifacts and memorabilia from that year's World's Fair. In fact, the original name for the organization was the Columbian Museum of Chicago. The building you see in this picture was not built until 1921 and is part of a campus of museums on the Chicago lakefront that includes the Shedd Aquarium and Adler Planetarium visible in the photo below. Prior to the new building's construction and the move north from Jackson Park, the collection was housed in the building known as the Art Palace.

In remembrance of the city fire, the World's Fair hosted Chicago Day to commemorate the tragedy of 1871. As you can see, thousands turned out that October 9th to the Grand Plaza to celebrate its recovery from the incident that destroyed so many homes and businesses.

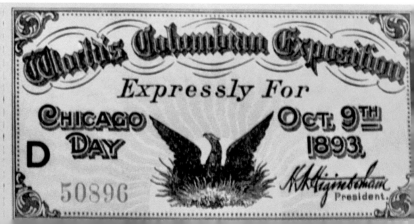

Before the official opening of the Exposition, a military parade was staged. In this engraving soldiers are making their way in front of the Transportation Building on October 21st of 1892 with temporary elements such as the wooden concessions buildings and bridge in the background. A lot of work still needed to be completed before opening day the following spring.

Staging such a large event creates a plethora of safety concerns. Emergency crews patrolled the grounds keeping attendees secure during swimming contests, fireworks displays, and even drilled on fire fighting.

In fact, a fire did break out during the Exposition. A cold storage warehouse ignited on July 10th of 1893 killing a number of firemen in the conflagration while approximately 50,000 people were on the grounds.

In total, millions of people passed through the gates into the Columbian Exposition. Thousands were in Jackson Park daily, the Columbian Guard was on-hand to help in the event of safety issues around the park. However, they had little true authority and many were "decommissioned" in the middle of the Fair's run.

As deadlines closed in, selecting a color scheme for the structures and attractions became a pressing issue to solve. Color Department Superintendent Allen decided to mask the city in white.

Here a team prepares to hose down an exterior wall to save an incredible amount of time. This was one of the first uses of a "paint gun" in history and reduced the number of man-hours necessary to make sure buildings were dressed for opening day.

Architecture & Grounds

Architects and designers from all over the world contributed to the edifices that created the internationally eclectic skyline of structures in Jackson Park during the Expo

Buildings became literal canvases to not only the paint crews but also the men tasked with cobbling together ideas to express with materials that were classic, indigenous, and new to the era. Materials science had advanced considerably throughout the 1800's. The dominance of iron gave way to the prevalence of steel after Henry Bessemer patented his process to aid in removing impurities.

While it's certainly true that classic forms were ubiquitous, they were often just a facade - only as deep as the visible layer. Beneath the paint and plaster was a different story. It was steel and electric light that made many of the structures viable to the crowds, as was the case for the Manufactures Building.

The Administration Building was centrally located and featured an octagonal dome, making it easy to identify since few others had a similar feature. Architecturally the structure also had columns that historians and architects would refer to as Doric & Ionic, terminology also familiar to musicians working through the modal scales.

The view from the dome of the Administration Building must have been impressive. The opportunity to get a sprawling, bird's eye view of any area in the late 19th century was a novelty.

Even the Ferris Wheel can be seen faintly in the distance from the balcony, which illustrates the scale of the event's footprint on the south side of Chicago.

Today we take electricity and lightbulbs for granted - however, in the Gilded Age they were both still luxuries that demonstrated state-of-the-art advances in science and technology. Below we see the Administration Building artificially illuminated in the night for audiences.

Inscribed on the the Peristyle are the words: "Ye shall know the truth and the truth shall make you free". This is the view from the inside of the event, though the Peristyle itself also had a face to Lake Michigan. It served as a marine entrance, allowing boats to pass in and out of Jackson Park.

This image is the Colonnade of the Peristyle leading to the Music Hall. Though only half is shown, the entire run of columns was 600' long, height and width being 60' each.

"The Court of Honor" included many of the feature elements that are shown in greater detail throughout this collection of photos.

The heroic Statue of "The Republic" stood 65' tall and was coated in a layer of gold leaf. Imagine this scene in the eyes of the day, a glistening embodiment of the Gilded Age in the U.S. There was no shortage of artistic opulence throughout the Chicago Fair.

Could you imagine it gleaming in the sunlight? As fate would have it, the sculptor Daniel Chester French completed a 24' replica which was placed on the former area the Grand Basin to commemorate the city's 100th anniversary.

The Transportation building cut a distinct style amongst the other large structures. The ostensibly recursive portal in this first picture was done in a red theme, directly contrasting the stoic white throughout the park during the Expo.

The Transportation "portal" was a beautiful entrance, elaborate and functionally a visual wonder. So much so that attendees could regularly be heard asking "Have you seen that Golden Doorway?"

Each side of the portal entrance was also bookended by a pair of overlooks. Ornate and intricate, these sections of the buildings as well as the rest of the structure stood in opposition to the predominately classical forms in the park.

The Art Palace, a work of art itself, was designed by Chicago architect C. B. Atwood. The dome stands 125' high, while the inside originally had 150 rooms and displayed artists from 20 countries. Can you say *"epic scale"*? Just imagine the White City in full bloom, it wasn't even the biggest building on the grounds.

This is the Art Palace on the lagoon side. Perhaps it looks familiar? It is still in active use! If modern visitors could travel back to the summer of 1893, they would recognize it as the Museum of Science & Industry. The only structure erected with the intention of outlasting the White City after the Fair closed.

The Palace of Mechanic Arts has symbolic meaning from the mathematics of antiquity layered into the building's facade. Classical figures and design were the brilliant efforts of artists and architects from around the U.S. and beyond.

As shown on the opposing page, the Mechanic Arts Building was adorned with many statues. These images are views of the entire structure as well as the statues placed atop the Palace.

Pictured here is the Midway Plaisance viewed from the Western Entrance before the Captive Balloon was damaged in harsh weather. The Midway was where visitors had access to the wide variety of concessions and attractions found in the White City.

The two cities of Chicago and Pittsburgh share an industrial history that reaches back to the time of the railroads at least. There is no better physical expression of their connectedness than the Ferris Wheel which debuted in the White City after being manufactured in the Steel City. In fact, Chicago has a wheel to this day in Navy Pier, though the legacy of its creator was not as enduring. He died just a few years later. However, the original wheel was erected two more times. It operated for a number of years in the Lincoln Park neighborhood of Chicago before relocating to St. Louis for the World's Fair held in 1904.

On a trip through Pittsburgh, where the large steel components of the wheel were manufactured, I had the opportunity to visit the convention center and captured this picture of a miniaturized replica of the Ferris Wheel.

Burnham Plan

Many residents and students of architecture are familiar with the legacy that Daniel Burnham left behind in the city of Chicago and beyond the metropolis through his works. The large green space that buffers "The Loop" in Chicago and Lake Michigan is known as Grant Park. Formally securing this space for future citizens goes back to the design manual he produced for the Second City referred to as "The Burnham Plan". However, the green space goes back to the founding of the city and was defended in court numerous times by Aaron Montgomery Ward.

This site is now home to the world-class installation known as Millenium Park, which is equal parts cosmopolitan park, art gallery, and performance space. Perhaps the most recognized emblem of this public amenity is Cloudgate, colloquially called "the Bean", a massive polished stainless steel sculpture that resembles a jelly bean.

Crown Fountain is equal parts fountain, splash pad, and staring contest. The two glass structures have faces showing on the interior surfaces from video clips. They express looks of happiness and will periodically purse their lips into a kissing formation at which point a considerable stream of water is emitted from the location of the mouth.

The final major structural feature created during the park's construction is the open air amphitheater called Pritzker Pavilion. This venue hosts concerts and other performances through the months when the weather is conducive to outdoor events in a city that appreciates when it isn't winter.

Millennium Park is an amazing installation that connects the city's history of world-class experiences to present-day use habits for the constant influx of visitors that to the city.

Metropolitan downtown centers often exhibit a character that makes them uniquely identifiable. The best way to symbolically communicate that is with a panoramic photograph of a city's skyline.

Lake Michigan is a special feature that forms the city's eastern boundary. The massive natural resource was as revered in the Gilded Age as it is today. The committee in charge of producing the 1893 World's Fair in Chicago used the lake's location to secure Jackson Park which is adjacent to the fresh water lake on the south side of the city.

Navy Pier can be seen in the far right portion of the panoramic photo of the city's skyline on the previous page. The short, thin white strip jutting into the sky from the pier is a Ferris Wheel that takes riders high into the air for incredible views of downtown, Grant Park, and of course the pier itself.

More of the Grounds

The structural style of the Women's Building, referred to as Italian Renaissance, was considered austere in its detailing compared to many of the others and can be seen above. Notable for the era, the architectural design and management of the construction was overseen exclusively by prominent women.

This expression of inclusion was uncommon for the times. However, acts like these were the vanguard of the movement that ultimately secured the right to vote via the women's suffrage movement in the decades that followed. Social issues of this kind gained a lot of steam heading into the next century.

The Electricity Building housed wonders within that put visitors into awe during the Gilded Age. It cost a staggering $410k at the time of its construction, which converts to more than $11 million in today's money. For his initial experiments using a kite to research electricity, a statue of Benjamin Franklin was placed in the hemicycle (the inverted cylindrical and domed) entrance of the building as well as a place upon a limited number of admission tickets.

125 years ago the country was already known to have significant resource deposits throughout the land. The Mines and Mining Building showcased the technology being used by the industry at-large.

Whether it is ore-based metals or digital transactions, our mining industry and the monetary policy it facilitates remains a topic of discussion. It was no less vital in 1893. Only a few decades prior, the Gold Rush had changed the life course of many speculators that decided to go west and prospect for the precious metal.

Horticultural Hall was an elegant building with a glass dome allowing light to pass through to the benefit of the plants growing inside. Under the dome, plants and flowers of all kinds were on display with extensive cultural themes that also integrated electric lights and water features.

The Wooded Island was an outdoor respite from the constructed buildings and scenes of the World's Fair. Shrubs and grass covered the areas along with walking paths while trees offered shade coverage. The Horticultural Building, itself a storehouse of flora, can be seen in the distance.

Only a few buildings were permitted on the Wooded Island, one was the Hunter Cabin. The building replicated a typical homestead-style logged cabin that facilitated expansion across the frontier of North America. Teddy Roosevelt assisted with construction of the chimney, before he decided to formally enter a career in politics.

Christopher Columbus

Just as this statue of Christopher Columbus stood in the portico of the Administration Building to greet people coming inside, the Columbian Exposition ushered those visitors and the society at-large of the Gilded Age through the doorway of the 20th Century by introducing them to innovations of all kinds. The Industrial Revolution may have started to influence industry and commerce in significant ways in the decades prior, but it was this event that introduced many of those advances to the domestic lives of attendees.

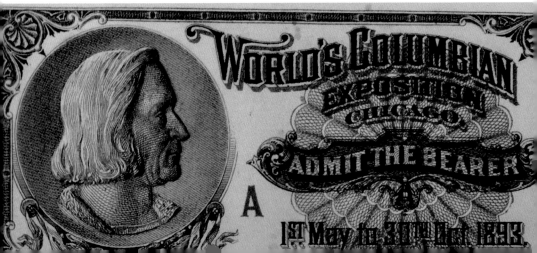

The legacy of Columbus stretched across the entirety of the 1893 World's Fair. The sculpture above, known as a quadriga due to its team of four horses, was an emblematic celebration of his efforts to explore the Americas. It was located on the Peristyle facing inwardly toward the Grand Basin, the sculpture can be seen in the other photos that show that feature next to the Court of Honor.

Additionally, a half dollar coin was struck by the U.S. Mint which depicted Columbus on its front - the first commemorative issue of its kind allowed by the government. As the primary namesake of the event, his likeness also graced a number of admission passes, which can be sen on the opposing page.

The Spanish government contributed replicas of the Santa Maria (pictured alone), Niña and Pinta which are seen together. Built in the Iberian country, they repeated the expedition to the Caribbean as had occurred 400 years prior before continuing on to their final destination in the White City by the lake.

Europe

The future was integral to many of the attractions but history was also a focal point. Columbus planned the transatlantic expedition while staying in Palos, Spain. Approximately four hundred years later the Convent of Rabida where he stayed was replicated for the Chicago attendees to gaze upon with their own eyes.

The Spanish Empire had been receding across the globe for quite some time by the late 1800's, though the nation was able to erect this building at the Columbian Exposition.

Within the decade the United States and Spain would be at war. However, it did have some level of prominence in Jackson Park as the country that financed the voyage of Columbus.

Germany unified into an empire just a few decades prior to the Exposition. Exhibiting in 1893 was an opportunity for prestige that the Bismarck didn't want to miss. The culture of the reorganized territories and their technical prowess were on display during the Fair via an incredible collection of art as well as military armaments.

The preparations necessary to execute the event were extensive, which is why it ultimately took place 401 years after Spain sent the first unintentional voyage to "the new world". The German building was extravagantly ornamented. It showcased the great wealth and design preferences of many classic German structures. In the photo above it is under construction before its final detailing was in place for the opening of the event.

Visitors marveled at the feats of engineering throughout the Exhibition, including the armaments manufactured for the Krupp gun exhibit. It was independent of the German national installations but were certainly associated with the military might of the empire.

They dwarfed any previous cannons casted, this fact alone made transporting them from Germany to Chicago an engineering feat in itself.

The Victoria Building was England's structural contribution to the Exposition. Sizable though it was, visitors were permitted little direct access to the interior which was a policy that was poorly received by the public. It also garnered a less than enthusiastic reception regarding its aesthetic qualities.

Queen Victoria would remain the regent of England until 1901. For the Exposition, a memorial for her late husband Prince Albert who had passed in 1861 was sculpted to represent the nation in stone. The statue to the right was a representation of "America" as it was shown on the original monument in Kensington Gardens which had depictions for "Africa", "Asia", and continental "Europe" as well.

There were two locations designated as the "Irish Village" but the one depicted in this engraving was known as "Blarney Castle". Unfortunately, this angle doesn't show that structure and we are only able to see the portal to enter the village itself where there was a museum, gift shops, and artisans.

The cost of exhibiting was high, thus booths became vending opportunities akin to an international trade show of cultures. The Austrian goods seen here were for sale to crowds of people looking for a souvenir to take home. In addition, many nations constructed a decorative facade inside the Manufactures Building, as can be seen from this Austrian example below.

Though the previous Fair had been hosted in Paris, France had a generally understated presence in 1893. However, the shadow of Eiffel reached across the Atlantic, spurring on the desire to create a feature that could compete with the iron monument erected four years prior. France's building (seen on the opposing page) was ornate and instructive, featuring demonstrations in the two wings and art within the central gallery.

The Norwegian's strived for authenticity when designing and constructing their building. Built in the Scandinavian country of Norway pine, it was deconstructed and shipped to Chicago for reassembly onsite. The gable flourishes are meant to emulate the bow of ancient Norse boats (below).

LIBERTÉ EGALITÉ FRATERNITÉ

Sweden's building was equally impressive architecturally to its fellow Scandinavian structure. Epic and unique, the building's style was emblematic of churches or castles found within the country approximately 200 years prior to its placement in Jackson Park. Unfortunately, an insurance issue closed it to the public in the latter days of the Exposition.

States

Great expanses of the country were cultivated by the late 1800's. Many areas that had been part of a large territorial development earned their statehood as people migrated there to make a life. Advances in food production via commercial and industrial developments were put front and center at the World's Fair by many participating states.

Inside the Illinois building was a mural made of grains like a mosaic. There were a number of artistic works depicted with grocer's wares throughout the state buildings, including pickles, oranges and others.

Since Chicago was the site of the fair, Illinois contributed $800k to the finances of the event - a vast sum back then which is equal to more than $22 million today. A quarter million of those dollars were used to create this impressive structure and its interior which highlighted the state.

Illinois is known as the "Land of Lincoln", his statue stands to this day in front of the statehouse as seen below. The era of "Reconstruction" focused the Union's effort to keep the country unified while attempting to put the states in the south back together following the war. By the close of the 19th century many communities had been cobbled back together from the destruction which had torn them apart. The country's sixteenth president was memorialized on an admission pass, as were a few other notable individuals.

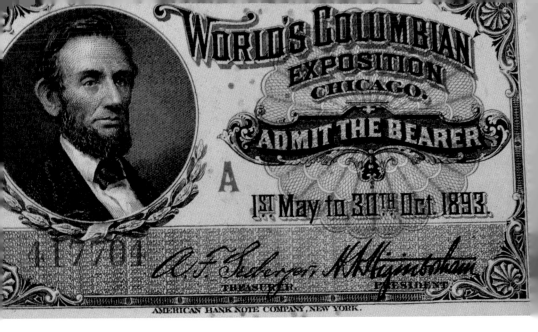

The grounds where the Columbian Exposition was staged became a city unto itself. In this image many state buildings can be seen with Illinois featuring most prominently, along with the pond of Jackson Park. Many states and countries had structures at the Exposition. Inside the majority of state-associated buildings were incredible showcases.

This is the California building, it resembled the Spanish mission architectural style that existed in the coastal state. These photos show the Statue of California to the right and orange displays as visitors would have seen in the building.

The World's Fair of 1893 was about featuring the fantastic, the lives we have beyond daily obligation. As poets and philosophers have expressed for centuries, the human spirit endures precisely because we find inspiration from the impressive achievements of creators. California embodied that spirit for many in the second half of the 19th century and is certainly still a part of its legacy to this day.

The Indiana building (above) had an almost Gothic tone to its design. It's fitting that the Hoosiers were ambitious in their construction if for no other reason than proximity to the Windy City, which is located in the next state to the West.

Throughout the grounds classical forms were ubiquitous, perhaps even preferred given how many builders opted to embrace that look. Architects of the Midwest understood the local climate and, as can be seen on the Michigan building (top right), affixed porches to their structures to give attendees a reprieve from outdoor conditions during the summer.

Wisconsin's building was created in a style of the era but done up with materials sourced from the great state itself: lumber and stone. Chicago's central location on the continent with amble rail extending into every direction made the delivery of goods an easier task in a time before automobiles and aircrafts.

Ohio's building (below) resembles the White House in basic terms, though far less extravagant given the intention to survive only through the World's Fair. An interesting note: Ohio chose to not include displays of the state's prowess and served as a clubhouse. The porches measured over 100' while the house itself was 50' deep, all built for $30,000.

Though the exterior of the New Jersey building was austere, once inside visitors were treated to a lavish interior. Particularly notable was a bedroom that replicated the one Gen. Washington used while garrisoned in Morristown. America's colonial history was still a significant mythological milestone for the young country, which had celebrated it's centennial in the late 1876.

Vermont's building (bottom right) embodied the ever present classical style showcased across the grounds in a number of ways, including the use of marble. A Roman-like courtyard of sculptures greeted visitors before entering the main structure. The statues which can be seen represented state industries that created its economy.

The Rhode Island building bares classic ornamentations born in antiquity to great effect and wouldn't be out of place amongst the industrialists' mansions of Newport. Smaller as it was compared to many of those constructed by other states, the cost to erect the structure was accordingly proportional at $7,000 - though it was still a great sum in those days.

In the years leading up to the Exposition, site selection was contested by two metropolises of the US - New York City and Chicago were in the hunt. Opinions may linger regarding which city truly deserved the honor, but it was the Windy City that won out. New York's ornate building (right) was highly regarded for its style.

As a sign of respect for the efforts put forth by the New York City delegation, Manhattan earned a day of celebration. Special tickets were issued for October 21st, 1893 with the image of the recently gifted Statue of Liberty on its face. Of course, in time the Big Apple would get its chance to answer back a few decades later with a pair of events in 1939-40 and 1964-65.

As the country was forming, Pennsylvania played a grand part and so has a revered history. The Keystone State's building (above) assembled for the event replicated the look of Independence Hall in Philadelphia. A crowd is present in this picture taken on Pennsylvania Day. It's said forty thousand people were in the park from the namesake state itself.

The Texas building was large like the formerly independent republic. Despite initial funding problems, the state was able to construct this structure for the Fair thanks to the efforts of resident ladies of the state who pressed to make sure it was represented. Its style clearly echoes typical construction of the Lone Star state and the Southwest in general. An architect from San Antonio won the honor to design it with authentic flair.

The Hawaiian exhibit centered around a replica of the volcano Kīlauea, though it had not yet achieved statehood. The monarchy that had ruled the islands was overthrown in 1893, which ultimately put it on the path toward eventual statehood as number 50.

The Louisiana building was modeled after those found on the streets of the French Quarter in New Orleans. Concessions and entertainment were in the fashion of the Crescent City as well. A Creole kitchen and concert company brought the sounds in addition to the tastes of the delta to Chicago. This trend continued through the 20th century as blues musicians worked the venue circuits between the two cities.

Nautical

Access to Lake Michigan was integral to not only site selection while planning the layout of the Fair but also served as a logistic resource. Thanks to the canals that were channeled into the swampy Jackson Park terrain, boats were able to travel through the Expo and ferry visitors between attractions.

It lent a Venetian atmosphere to the event as can be seen in this image of a gondola passing the Horticultural Building.

This ferry bore the namesake of the event - the *Christopher Columbus* was state-of-the-art for the time. It moved attendees from the city downtown at Van Buren St. to the Fair or in the opposite direction. However, though it's lean and narrow design was responsive on the water, those factors combined with conditions on the lake could result in seasickness for passengers.

A boat parade was held on September 9th of 1893. Mariners from around the globe showed off their water crafts for the crowd lined up along the canal's edge to catch a glimpse as they floated by that day.

The Exposition celebrated Columbus and his voyage to the lands that would be known as the Americas. Norway felt the legacy of the Vikings should have a presence at the World's Fair and so constructed then sailed this ship to the event. It is rumored that Columbus visited Iceland in 1477 where he heard stories of a distant land. Do you think that anecdote is myth or fact?

Before cars and planes changed the way people travel, boats moved goods and travelers across the waterways in great numbers. Maritime science allowed empires to stretch across the oceans and open trade routes as well as exploitation that defined European colonial efforts.

Protecting sea-lanes or harbors required vigilance as well as an array of technologies depicted below such as the model lighthouse and buoys seen in this collection.

Millions attended the Fair over the course of its run in Chicago and keeping the masses fed was vital. The city's large stockyard and meatpacking districts accommodated supply needs but it was concession buildings that went the last mile via cafeterias and dining halls inside the gates of the expo.

Café de la Marine (shown above), as it was fittingly called for its menu of fish and oyster offerings, was one of many eateries distributed amongst the other locations.

Attractions were prevalent throughout the Fair in Jackson Park. Inside this one was a massive diving demonstration tank where visitors could witness a diver underwater.

For many, this was not only their chance to see this technology but also the immense body of water known as Lake Michigan. Residents that live near the Great Lakes or coasts can forget how special their geographic placement is at times. It's important to remember how vast the open stretches of country are though the middle of the United States.

As was detailed previously, Chicago's proximity to Lake Michigan afforded the event an opportunity to embrace the aquatic nature of the voyage Columbus made and to display seafaring technologies too.

Battleship Illinois was a replica created from brick, built up from the lake bottom that allowed "passengers" to board and enter the "ship" to see what life was like aboard a naval vessel for themselves. A battleship like this would not be allowed on the Great Lakes according to treaty.

The Gilded Age was definable as an epoch of advancement comparable with any the world had seen before, and as the Krupp artillery exhibit illustrated earlier: weaponry was no exception.

Editorial notes below this engraving of the *Illinois* in the book of this photo collection included the sentiment "wars of the future must blanch even the faces of [its] inventors".

The Fisheries Building was equivalent to what we refer to as an "aquarium" these days. This structure displayed aquatic life as it had never been seen before in the Western Hemisphere, boasting three thousand square feet of viewable glass full of creatures like King Crab, anemones and rays.

While zoos were still fairly rare in the 1800's, aquariums were outright nonexistent. Novelist Jules Verne's books explored the mysteries of the world in the second half of the century. *20,000 Leagues Under the Sea* was only a few decades old by 1893 and sparked heavy interest in what existed beneath the currents.

International

Most of the established individual United States were present for the event and a few Native American Indian tribes were also represented. A number of replicated living spaces were recreated on the grounds for visitors to interact with too. The installation above reflects the domestic conditions the cliff-dwellers of Battle Rock Mountain Colorado. It cost 25 cents to take the tour.

While Native American Indians had a semblance of representation at Chicago's Fair, it was often merely totemic in depth. As the 19th century came to a close, the last battles of "cowboys and indians" were taking place in pockets across the country. Tokens of the vanishing West, Native people of North America were being sent to live on reservations that often didn't resemble the environments in which they had developed their way of life.

The dwellings in the picture below belonged to the Penobscots, who were pushed into a reservation in Maine during the era when it received statehood. Conflicting land claims have resulted in legal battles between many tribes and states. Meanwhile, the federal government is still sorting out how to interface with sovereign nations within its own borders to this day.

Brazil was one of the wealthiest nations in the world at the time of the first Chicago World's Fair. They showed up ready to convert that financial opulence into architecture.

This building was erected to celebrate the nation's standing. In addition to the central dome, it had four wings with two stories each. Sizable and ornate, the Brazilian's created a rival to some of the most grandiose state buildings that were present.

These are replicas of the ruins of Uxmal Archaeological news and stories were popular around the turn of the century. Ancient cultures around the world were regularly being rediscovered by excavation and research. These models from the Yucatán were created using papier-mâché in the depth of the jungles. They were manufactured by Edward H. Thompson and displayed in the Anthropological Building.

People have been fascinated by Egyptian culture for millennia and the late 19th century was no different. Discovery and conversion of the Rosetta Stone in the one hundred years prior set off a heavy interest in antiquities from the nation. In addition to a replicated "Street in Cairo" the Exhibition also featured a rendition of the Luxor Temple with obelisks.

The Columbian Exposition was a World's Fair and Daniel Burnham made every effort to ensure the event exhibited global class. International travel was an expensive proposition in those days, so bringing the world to Chicago created an opportunity to absorb worldly culture in ways that most people could never afford.

The Persian Palace was a cultural experience and occupied by residents of the land who traveled some of the longest routes to arrive in the White City.

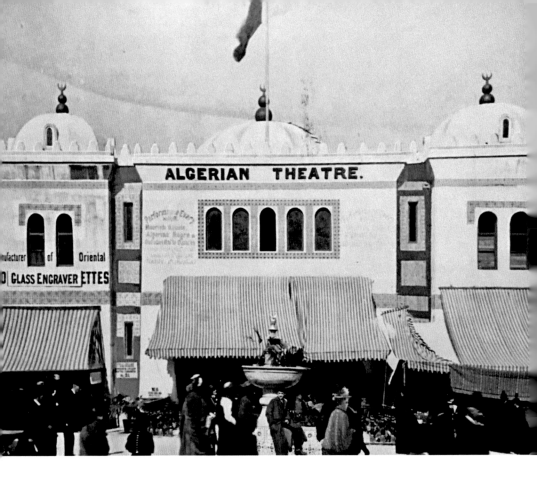

The Algerian Theatre was amongst the most successful concessions in Jackson Park during the World's Fair. It had dancing women, extreme displays of live body modification, and musical performances.

Despite lingering accusations to its authenticity regarding the representation of customs and culture of Algeria, even President Cleveland "visited" during his procession through the Midway.

The Building of India was beautifully ornate with detailed flourishes both inside and out. Visitors were embraced by the scent of sandalwood and could relax with tea after passing through the entrance you can see here that was comparable to that of the Transportation Portal.

The Chinese Theater was made possible by the Wah Mee Exposition Company. While the building's construction was handled by Chicago labor and may not look authentic, it did feature stage plays as well as fortune telling.

The country of Japan had a considerable presence at the Columbian Exposition, which is notable because the nation only opened their ports and communities to outsiders less than fifty years prior in 1854.

The Ho-o-den (which translates to Phoenix Temple) was dedicated in May 1893, a gift from the Mikado, and constructed by artisans of the nation. The Japanese installation was also located on the Wooded Island.

The Javanese settlement was large with enough room for an orchestra of musicians to perform. It consisted of stringed apparatuses, drums, xylophone-like instruments and a gong, all able to be heard at considerable distance from their performance area. The tonality was foreign to western ears, but was valued as a nice background soundtrack while walking the streets and paths.

This Bedouin family brought their Middle Eastern lifestyle to Chicago including weaponry, horses and the hookah which is visible next to the chief on the left. While the travel required for Americans to visit the Expo was long, it was vastly eclipsed by the distances required for international troupes to get to the south side.

The Ottoman Empire's history stretched for centuries by the late 1800's. However, it had never opted to participate in an Exhibition with the West. That changed in Chicago when they staged this structure and displayed a vast collection of cultural artifacts. In only a few short decades the lands claimed by the Ottomans would no longer exist as a unified whole.

Arts

The producers of the Exposition intended for art to be prevalent inside Jackson Park. Sculptural works like these angels were constructed and distributed judiciously. The large outdoor areas and expansive buildings allowed for flourishes in impressionist conceptualizations alongside ornate exterior detailing.

These photos show the Statue of Industry (Top Left) and the Statue of Plenty (Top Right) looking over the Great Basin. Between the two is the Statue of the Republic, which can be seen in a number of photos of the Court of Honor. Visitors would come by this massive body of water to visit the feature buildings that were centrally located and close to train access.

A pair of statues known as "Proctor's Cowboy & Indian" were located near the Golden Door of the Transportation Building, if you can recall the building with the arched doorway. His work was considered some of the finest at the Exhibition. A.P. Proctor's sculptural legacy can be found all over the country, and his contributions during his era are still renowned.

This sculptural piece is known as *Horoscopes*, it has a lot of great directional symbolism relating to the globe as well as the Zodiac. Layering mythological themes into art was a popular trend in the late 1800's, perhaps to suggest a timeless connection to antiquity.

The Farmer's Bridge allowed visitors to pass between the Machinery Building and Agricultural Hall toward the south end of the Great Basin. There was a visual embellishment of one kind or another located at nearly predictable intervals wherever people could walk. Also in view in this image is Neptune on the spire and many of the sculptures distributed across the grounds.

Notice additionally the sculpture *Horoscopes* from the previous page atop the building in the mid-ground of the engraving on this one.

Modern cement was only developed and refined over the last few centuries. That process and the innovations in construction it allowed were still novel in the second half of the 1800's. When combined with steel, these two assets allowed construction to realize designs that reached for the sky. Popular sculptural pieces were replicated in concrete for the audiences in Chicago who would otherwise be unlikely to see the originals with their own eyes.

Artistic works were not only present outdoors but also inside many galleries that displayed pieces from all over the world. This one featured sculpture and paintings from France, the host of the previous World's Fair in 1889.

Not to be outdone by the previous World's Fair host and continental rival, Germany's Bismarck dispatched a large collection for display. As can be seen from the collection of photos highlighting the nation, its leaders were eager to exhibit prestige in Chicago and illustrate that it was truly a cultural force in the late 19th century.

The Fair wasn't just about wondrous sights, tastes, and first-time experiences like riding Ferris's Wheel but also sounds from around the world. Global languages and music representing culture from every continent where men had developed society were present. American composer John Phillips Sousa wrote a piece of music to commemorate the run of the 1893 Columbian Exposition titled *The Liberty Bell*. If you have ever watched the British sketch comedy show *Monty Python's Flying Circus*, the song will be familiar as the theme used to open the program.

Attractions

Despite the efforts to prohibit alcohol and nudity by temperance-minded women in advance of the World's Fair, the event embraced the bawdy. This structure was allowed to feature beauties from around the globe and scantily-clad belly dancers could be found as well.

Because of the adjacent large body of water, Chicago can facilitate marinas and large piers that reach into Lake Michigan for commercial, industrial, and recreational purposes. Modern day visitors to Chicago are familiar with Navy Pier, but the city has a history of notable piers dating back to the Columbian Exposition.

The structure allowed for boat traffic to disembark at the World's Fair and let tired guests relax on the mechanized chair path that ran its length. However, it ultimately broke midway through the six-month run of the Fair and wasn't repaired due to expense.

World's Fair organizers felt an emblem of the event should be manufactured to commemorate it. Colonial and Revolutionary era artifacts were contributed from across the country to combine with bronze. This new *Liberty Bell* toured through New York City, Philadelphia, Pittsburgh, and Indianapolis on its way to Chicago.

The John Bull locomotive was already more than 50 years old by the time of the Columbian Exposition. It journeyed from Jersey City to be available for visitors to see at the event. Transportation was crossing the last frontiers of the United States rapidly as the 20th century approached.

The Windy City is a nickname long held by Chicago. Regardless of the origins, participants felt it was a good opportunity to play on the phrase and so a variety of windmills were contributed from around the globe. As you can see from this image of the collection, there was a good variety of contributions. The people of 1893 were as interested in viewing the movement of celestial bodies as those from any time before or since.

For the Expo, the Yerkes Telescope was constructed at the cost of $500,000, which at the time was the biggest in the world. After its time in Chicago, the massive instrument was relocated to Lake Geneva, Wisconsin where it continued operating via funding from the University of Chicago until October of 2018.

Attendees could enjoy all sorts of shows and concessions on the Midway. The ostriches were a popular attraction. They were available to view for only 10 cents. Food dishes were also sourced and created from the animals for special occasions.

Legacy

It's clear from these photographs that Chicago's Columbian Exposition was a one-of-a-kind event that drew on the imaginations of the country's best structural artists. The fading Western wilderness and completion of "Manifest Destiny" were replaced with a new vision of "American Exceptionalism" that placed the nation's identity into the world's consciousness. It also left an impression on the imaginations of visitors, many who went home inspired by the cornucopia of industrial and commercial products gathered to Jackson Park in 1893.

Unfortunately, an attempt to bring another World's Fair to Chicago in 1992 for the 500th anniversary of Columbus crossing the Atlantic failed to get off the ground. It would have made the lakefront adjacent to Grant Park downtown into a combination of lagoons and "floating" attractions. While that would have been an amazing event, it's partner Expo in Sevilla, Spain was held to great acclaim. As a child my family visited the site and I have a few memories which include the mascot Curro as well as my first laser tag experience.

This caliber of project is an inspiration, not only for those involved with its creation but also for those that gaze in wonder at the incredible feats of beauty whether they are in design or philosophical. Notable attendees include Henry Ford as well as Helen Keller along with Dr. Alexander Graham Bell and his wife. Walt Disney's father was a construction worker for the fair while living in Chicago, which Erik Larson posits in his book *The Devil in the White City* was a thematic inspiration for Walt by way of anecdote from his father.

There was no shortage of "firsts" catalogued during the Fair's run. The United States *Pledge of Allegiance* was debuted, along with the first commemorative coins and stamps issued by the U.S. Mint and Post office Department, respectively. Brand name products such as Juicy Fruit, Pabst Blue Ribbon, Vienna Beef, Quaker Oats, Shredded Wheat, and Aunt Jemima were introduced to consumers, altering the palette and dining room tables of Americans. While these hallmarks of the 20th century were present at the Columbian Exposition, it was attendees' appreciation for them that resulted in their finding a market and ultimately recognition as edible American culture.

People crave progress, to peer around the corner of the future and see what is soon to greet them before others have the opportunity to become familiar. Early adopters advance our culture by encouraging creative minds to continue developing their novel offerings. Landing upon a successful idea often means failing through a great number of bad ones along the way but we cannot be afraid of the difficulties on the path to discovery. We must encourage each other to try new things, so that we continue to have an increase in diverse and new experiences in which creativity is not shunned but instead able to flourish.

Photo Attributions

John Phillips Sousa's Band - Public Domain

All event photos - "The Dream City" 1893

Color Photos - Michael Finney

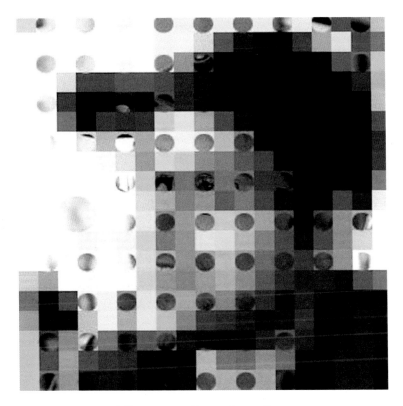

About the Author

Michael Finney is a full-spectrum content producer from the Midwest. He has explored music, audio, video, photography, and writing over a twenty year career that has taken him across the United States and beyond. Michael has provided the skills required for media production to a wide range of clients in many industries as an independent contractor. Additionally, he has a deep interest in technology and has worked within the telecommunications industry in a variety of roles.

Also Available from Michael Finney

Exploring Our National Parks Volume 1

How to Create a Personal Brand in 10 Steps

Made in United States
Orlando, FL
27 November 2022

25067391R00066